Our King Charles

For Sara and Josh
E.G.

For Grandma
R.G.

First published in Great Britain in 2023 by Wren and Rook

Paperback ISBN: 978 1 5263 6608 5
E-book ISBN: 978 1 5263 6609 2

1 3 5 7 9 10 8 6 4 2

Printed in the United Kingdom

Wren and Rook
An imprint of
Hachette Children's Group
Part of Hodder and Stoughton
Carmelite House, 50 Victoria Embankment
London EC4Y 0DZ

An Hachette UK Company
www.hachette.co.uk
www.hachettechildrens.co.uk

Our King Charles

HIS REMARKABLE JOURNEY FROM PRINCE TO KING

ELEANOR GREY

ROSE GERRARD

wren & rook

The new King Charles III

Back in the 1950s, there was a boy called Charles
who would grow up to be king of the United Kingdom.
Little did he know that he would wait 70 years to take the job.

King Charles's mother, Queen Elizabeth II, was the United Kingdom's *LONGEST-REIGNING* monarch. In June 2022 she celebrated her *SEVENTIETH YEAR* as queen! She died on 8 September the same year, and the country was very sad to say goodbye to such a beloved monarch.

The same day, Charles assumed the throne and became *KING CHARLES III*.

At 73, he is the oldest person to ever take the British throne. He is also British history's longest '*HEIR APPARENT*' – which means the next person to take the throne. King Charles didn't spend all that time doing nothing though. He spent his years finding and supporting different causes, while learning how to be a good monarch from his mother.

Over **250,000 PEOPLE** queued to see the Queen lying in state the week before the funeral. The queue was more than 16 kilometres long and it was constantly moving.

Some people queued for longer than **24 HOURS** to pay their respects to the Queen!

Young Charles

Charles was destined to be king as soon as he was born!

On 14 November 1948, Princess Elizabeth and Philip, Duke of Edinburgh, celebrated the birth of their first child, Charles. When Charles was only three years old, his grandfather, King George VI died, his mother became queen and Charles became heir apparent. That's a lot to happen in just one day!

Charles became a *BIG BROTHER* to Princess Anne in 1950. They have been very close since they were little. Ten years later, Prince Andrew was born, with Prince Edward following four years later.

Charles's grandmother was known as the *QUEEN MOTHER*. He loved her dearly – she introduced him to one of his great passions: music. She gave him lots of cuddles too!

In 1957, Charles became the first heir ever to go to *SCHOOL* outside of the palace. He never liked school very much. He was a dreamy child who loved drawing and painting. He went to Gordonstoun School in Scotland, where his father Philip had gone before him.

He struggled to make friends at school, but he did discover his love of acting. He even played the lead role in Macbeth in 1965, and the Queen was in the audience cheering him on!

Charles hated Gordonstoun. He had to wear shorts all year round and the windows were always open, even in winter!

The longest heir

King Charles is the longest-serving HEIR APPARENT in British history.
He kept very busy for those 70 years.

Charles was named heir apparent when his grandfather King George VI died on 6 February 1952.

After finishing school, Charles went to *CAMBRIDGE UNIVERSITY* and became the first heir to receive a bachelor's degree. He studied archaeology, anthropology and history.

Charles officially became *PRINCE OF WALES* on 1 July 1969 at his '*INVESTITURE*' – a big ceremony at Caernarfon Castle in Wales. He learnt Welsh especially for his speech.

From 1971 to 1976, Charles followed in his father's and grandfather's footsteps by serving in the *NAVY*.

On 29 July 1981, Charles married his first wife, Lady Diana Spencer, in a lavish ceremony at St Paul's Cathedral that was called 'the wedding of the century'. Over **750 MILLION PEOPLE** watched it across the world, making it the biggest televised wedding ever!

Charles and Diana celebrated the birth of their son **WILLIAM** on 21 June 1982. In 1984, their second son, **HARRY**, was born.

Sadly, Charles and Diana divorced after fifteen years of marriage. Tragedy then struck on 31 August 1997 when Diana was killed in a car crash in Paris.

On 9 April 2005, Charles married his second wife **CAMILLA**, who became the Duchess of Cornwall.

In a wedding almost as big as Charles and Diana's, Prince William married **KATE MIDDLETON** on 29 April 2011. Two years later, Charles's first grandchild, **PRINCE GEORGE**, was born on 22 July 2013.

Becoming King

Charles became king automatically when his mother died, but countries like to celebrate new kings and queens properly and they do this at a big event called a CORONATION.

The Crowns

There are two crowns at a coronation. There is the *Imperial State Crown*, which is the 'working' crown worn at major events, and *St Edward's Crown*, which is only used to crown a new king or queen during a coronation ceremony.

Traditionally, a new king or queen is given several fancy things to wear and hold throughout the coronation . . .

The Rod with the Dove

The Stole

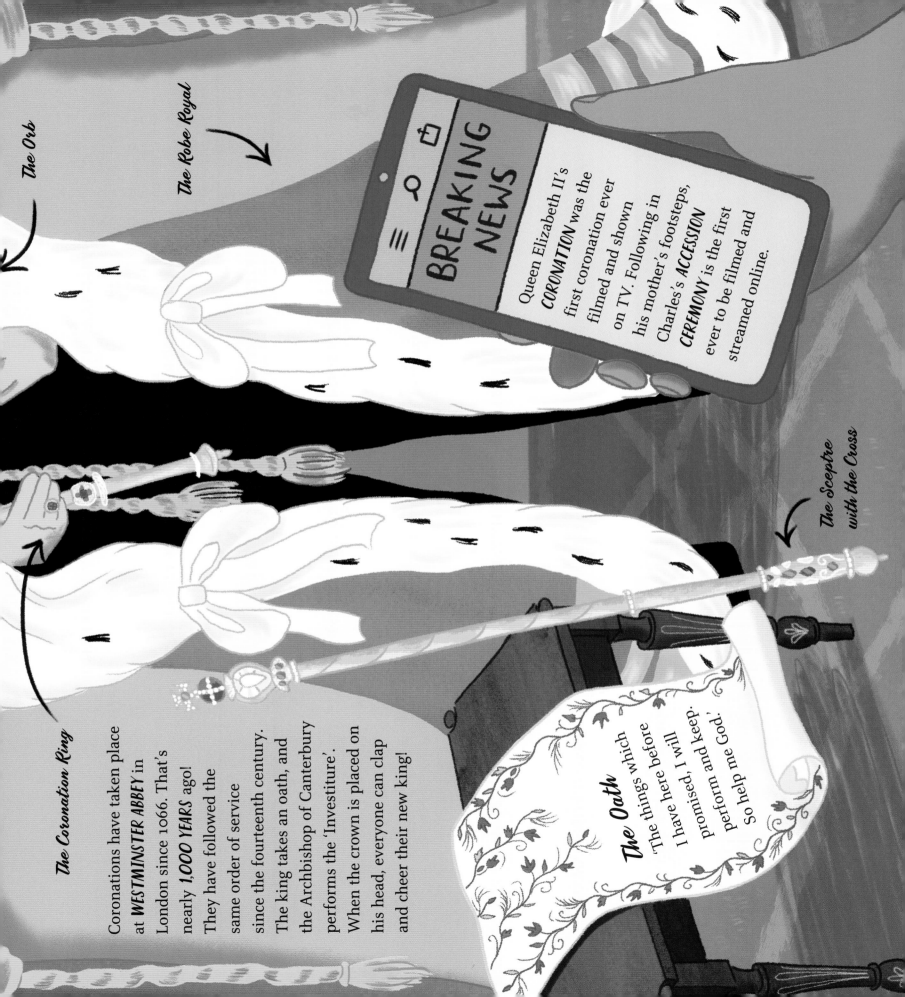

The Orb

The Robe Royal

The Coronation Ring

The Sceptre with the Cross

BREAKING NEWS

Queen Elizabeth II's *CORONATION* was the first coronation ever filmed and shown on TV. Following in his mother's footsteps, Charles's *ACCESSION CEREMONY* is the first ever to be filmed and streamed online.

Coronations have taken place at *WESTMINSTER ABBEY* in London since 1066. That's nearly *1,000 YEARS* ago! They have followed the same order of service since the fourteenth century. The king takes an oath, and the Archbishop of Canterbury performs the 'Investiture'. When the crown is placed on his head, everyone can clap and cheer their new king!

The Oath which
'The things which
I have here before
I have promised and keep.
promised and keep.
perform and keep.
So help me God.'

The King's family

King Charles's family is one of the most FAMOUS families in the world!

King Charles's wife Camilla is now the **QUEEN CONSORT.** Consort is the proper name for a royal 'wife' or 'companion'. Charles and Camilla had met and dated when they were young, but then married other people. They got back together and married in 2005.

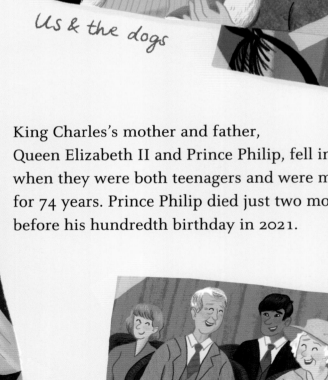

Holiday 2007

GREETINGS

Us & the dogs

Mother & Father on their wedding day

King Charles's mother and father, Queen Elizabeth II and Prince Philip, fell in love when they were both teenagers and were married for 74 years. Prince Philip died just two months before his hundredth birthday in 2021.

Mother & me at the rac

As Charles's oldest child, Prince William will be the **NEXT KING**. William met his wife Kate when they were at university together. They have three children, Prince George, Princess Charlotte and Prince Louis. William and Kate have many duties and their family often accompany them on tours and to official events. They are not always working though – the family is often seen being silly together!

Summer 2019

The Wedding of Harry & Meghan

Harry & Meghan's wedding, May 2018

Invictus Games, 2017

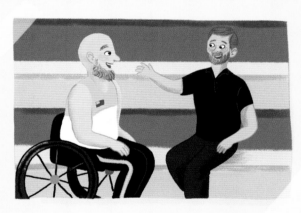

Prince Harry married his love, **MEGHAN**, in 2018. Harry and Meghan share a passion for activism. Harry founded the **INVICTUS GAMES** – a sporting event for injured and sick soldiers – while Meghan has dedicated her time to fighting for equality for all. When they're not campaigning, they're raising their two children, Archie and Lilibet (named after Queen Elizabeth), in California, USA.

A new face on every stamp

Everyone knows the Queen's portrait because it is on every bank note, coin and stamp in the country! The King's portrait will be just as famous one day.

The **NATIONAL ANTHEM** changed from 'God Save the Queen' to 'God Save the King' immediately. Crowds were heard **SINGING** it outside Buckingham Palace the day the Queen died. It's often heard before England or Northern Ireland play football matches!

Even as technology continues to develop, nothing can replace the importance of the postal system. The Queen's **ROYAL CYPHER** – a little picture of her initials with a crown – is on many post boxes in the UK and her portrait is on **EVERY STAMP**. These post boxes will remain on the street but when they need replacing, new ones will bear the King's cypher. The King's portrait will appear on stamps when the current stamps run out.

It used to be only royals who appeared on stamps. The first **NON-ROYAL** on a stamp was the playwright **WILLIAM SHAKESPEARE** in 1964.

In 2022, the Bank of England revealed King Charles's portrait which will appear on bank notes in 2024. The Royal Mint will add new coins to circulation with the King's portrait as they are needed.

The King's portrait appeared first on a special 50 pence coin in honour of the Queen's life.

Charles the Eco-King

The King has always loved the natural world, from farming his own food at home to speaking out to protect the whole planet!

In 1970, when Charles was 21, he gave a passionate speech about the *ENVIRONMENTAL CRISIS* the world was facing. A lot of people thought he was quite odd to care so much about *NATURE*. In fact, he'd even been spotted talking to plants and giving tree branches a friendly shake hello!

King Charles has never given up on helping the planet and doing what he believes is right, and now he is seen as one of the environment's most famous *ADVOCATES*.

King Charles believes that 'nature is our best teacher'. Over the last 50 years, he has been a royal patron for over **400 ENVIRONMENTAL ORGANISATIONS**, made speeches at climate change events and written to politicians encouraging their support for environmental policies.

A king's top eco-friendly tips!

King Charles tries to eat sustainably by eating less dairy, meat and fish.

The King loves his Aston Martin car. He made a special sustainable fuel for it using old wine and cheese whey – which is a kind of lumpy milk that gets wasted when cheese is made.

King Charles used nature to power the homes he lived in as a prince. He has a **HYDROELECTRIC TURBINE** at Birkhall in Scotland and **SOLAR PANELS** at Clarence House in London. Maybe Buckingham Palace could be solar-powered one day!

What's in a name...

King Charles doesn't have one name, but four — Charles Philip Arthur George. But he only got to pick one REGNAL name to be king. King Charles picked his Christian name, just like his mother picked hers.

Charles became the third king of his name, making him King Charles III. He follows in the footsteps of *TWO* other Charles, who led very different lives.

The first Charles had an unhappy reign, as *CIVIL WAR* broke out between Royalists (people who supported having a royal family) and Parliamentarians, who wanted to get rid of the monarchy.

OLIVER CROMWELL

The civil war didn't end well for poor Charles, whose reign ended when he was beheaded in 1649. The next 11 years were the only time that England did not have a king or queen – which made the country a 'republic'. Oliver Cromwell, who fought for the Parliamentarians and even signed Charles's death warrant, became Lord Protector of England.

King Charles I
(1600-1649)

King Charles II
(1630-1685)

King George VI
(1895-1952)

Some people thought King Charles might choose George for his regnal name in honour of his grandfather. King George VI was actually called *ALBERT*. He chose the name George, like his father, to give the people a sense of continuity after his brother decided not to be king.

After his father was beheaded, the second Charles lived in exile while England was a republic. Luckily for him, the republic failed. He was invited back to England and the public rejoiced to have a king again. He is known as the *MERRY MONARCH* and is considered one of the most popular kings. He had no children when he died and his throne passed to his brother, James.

A new royal pet!

The Queen had her corgis, but the King has his own favourite royal dog . . . the Jack Russell!

King Charles and Camilla have two Jack Russells called **BLUEBELL AND BETH**. Before Charles and Camilla adopted them, Beth was found abandoned and tied to a post and poor Bluebell was wandering the woods with no fur left. Now, they are the **FIRST RESCUE DOGS** to ever live in Buckingham Palace and they are very happy about it indeed!

Bluebell and Beth were rescued by **BATTERSEA DOGS AND CATS HOME,** which has been rescuing and rehoming animals since 1860.

The King has always loved
JACK RUSSELLS. Tigga was
Charles's constant companion
for all 18 years of his doggy life.
He was very popular and made it on to
several of the royal family Christmas cards.

The King's other favourite animal is the chicken. He has
his own chickens and feeds them and collects eggs from
them every morning. His grandchildren share his love
of chickens and one of his homes, Highgrove, has
a special nickname – *CLUCKINGHAM PALACE!*

A front row seat to history

King Charles has witnessed some of the biggest events in history throughout his time as heir.

1979: Margaret Thatcher became the first-ever **WOMAN** to be UK prime minister. She was also the UK's longest-serving prime minister, but she wasn't popular with everyone. Since then, we've had two more women prime ministers – Theresa May and Liz Truss.

1948: The **NATIONAL HEALTH SERVICE** was set up after the Second World War. The NHS means anyone can see a doctor or a nurse for free. The UK is very thankful to the NHS, especially for everything the doctors and nurses did for us during the COVID-19 pandemic.

1948

1979

1990

1987

1987: The General Election of 1987 was historic as it saw four Black members of parliament elected to the House of Commons. They were **DIANNE ABBOTT, PAUL BOATENG, BERNIE GRANT** and **KEITH VAZ.** Dianne Abbott was the first Black woman to become an MP and she's still an MP to this day.

2012: Great Britain hosted the Olympics in 2012 and the whole country got active. *MO FARAH* won double gold, *ANDY MURRAY* became the first British tennis player to win gold and the Queen even 'parachuted' into the stadium with *JAMES BOND!*

1990-2000: The 1990s were the years of '*GIRL POWER*' and in 1997 Prince Charles met Britain's biggest girl power popstars – *THE SPICE GIRLS!* Everyone around the world partied and celebrated on 1 January 2000 as we welcomed the turn of the century and a new millennium.

2000

2012

2014: In March 2014 it became legal for gay couples to celebrate their love and get *MARRIED.* The prime minister at the time, David Cameron, said: 'When people's love is divided by law, it is the law that needs to change.' Rainbow flags were waved as people flocked to be the first couples to be wed!

2014

2022

2022: In June 2022 the country and the world beyond celebrated the Queen's Platinum Jubilee, marking 70 years of her reign. There were four days of celebrations, from a parade and a pageant to the longest-ever street party!

The duties of a king

While the government looks after most of the running of the country,
Charles still has a very big job to do as King!

It's very important that the king knows what is happening in the country and he has *WEEKLY MEETINGS* with the prime minister to find out. These meetings are entirely private and while the king can't tell the prime minister what to do, he can listen and provide advice.

After a general election, the king invites the leader of the winning party to form a government in his name. Charles welcomed a new prime minister, *RISHI SUNAK*, in his first few months of being king.

Part of the job of being a monarch is to **TRAVEL**. If you added up all the Queen's trips, she would have made it around the world **OVER 40 TIMES!** King Charles is embarking on a world tour to 'extend a hand of friendship' following the death of his mother.

It's traditional for kings and queens to be '*POLITICALLY NEUTRAL*', which means they don't tell the government what to do. As heir, Charles was very passionate about politics and activism, but as king, he will have to follow the rules of his role.

ACT NOW

PROTECT THE

SAVE

SAVE THE TIGERS

Head of the Commonwealth

King Charles is the third head of the Commonwealth. The Commonwealth is an international association of independent countries, most of which used to be part of the British Empire.

The role of king is inherited, but the Head of Commonwealth role is not. In 2018, the Commonwealth leaders declared that Charles would be the next Head of the Commonwealth. There is no time limit on the role, so he will likely have it for the rest of his life.

The role is a **CEREMONIAL** one – the British monarch is not a ruler of the 54 member states of the Commonwealth. As such, there are no specific duties for the role, but Queen Elizabeth II was committed to feeling connected with the Commonwealth. In her time, she visited all but two Commonwealth nations in nearly 200 trips! Charles has toured the Commonwealth many times as heir and continues to as king.

The Commonwealth Realm

Charles isn't king of the Commonwealth countries, but he is 'head of state' – a ceremonial position – of 15 countries that together are called the Commonwealth Realm. They are Antigua and Barbuda, Australia, Belize, Canada, Grenada, Jamaica, New Zealand, Papua New Guinea, Saint Kitts and Nevis, Saint Lucia, Saint Vincent and the Grenadines, Solomon Islands, The Bahamas, Tuvalu and the United Kingdom.

The **COMMONWEALTH GAMES** are held every four years and 72 nations take part. Charles represented the Queen at the last Commonwealth Games in 2022, and read out her message that was placed in the Queen's baton. The baton travelled across **ALL 72 NATIONS!**

Giving back

King Charles has always been passionate about helping others.

The King is patron of more than **400 CHARITIES** and over the last 40 years he personally founded 15 charities as the Prince of Wales. These are called The Prince's Charities. Together they raise over **£100 MILLION** a year in the UK and overseas. Imagine how many people that money helps!

The Prince's Trust is one of the largest of the charities, supporting children and young adults in finding education and work in the UK, while the Prince's Trust International operates in more than 21 countries. Since it was founded, the charity has changed the lives of **OVER A MILLION** young people!

The King is also passionate about building **SUSTAINABLE** communities.

The crowning jewel of his charity the Prince's Foundation is Dumfries House. This stately home was on the brink of ruin until Charles restored it and opened it to the public. It offers training programmes for children in farming, science and arts as well as many fun events for the local community and beyond.

A new king for a new era

It's been over **70** years since the UK has had a new monarch
and a lot has changed in that time.

When Queen Elizabeth II was coronated
in 1953, the country was still adjusting
to life after the *SECOND WORLD WAR*.
TVs were in black and white, there
was *NO INTERNET* and no social media!
The world has changed more in the
last 70 years than in any other period
of history – from the invention of the
computer and sending rovers to Mars to
the continuing fight for equal rights for all.

At the age of 73, King Charles brings a lifetime of experience with him to the role of king. He's spent his life helping people, exploring his passions for art and music, raising an ever-growing family and speaking up for our planet.

KING CHARLES
CORONATION

STREET PARTY
6/5/23

As we enter a new era without the Queen, we look forward to the future and all that the King might achieve. But we also look to the past, at all he has done and the *INCREDIBLE LEGACY* of his mother. A legacy which he will hold in his heart and carry on his shoulders so that her memory will live on and guide him into the future. God save the King!